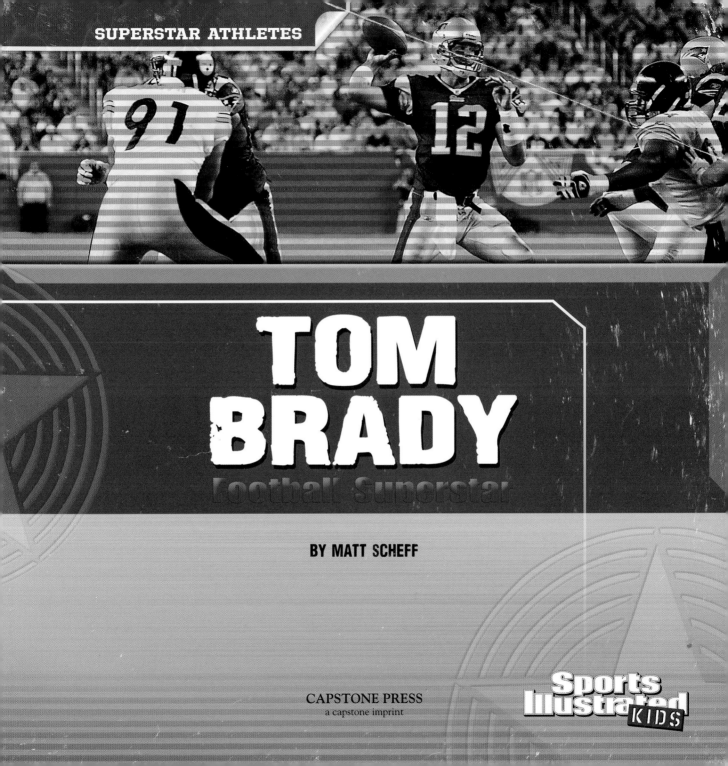

TOM BRADY

Football Superstar

BY MATT SCHEFF

CAPSTONE PRESS

a capstone imprint

Sports Illustrated KIDS

Sports Illustrated KIDS Superstar Athletes is published by Capstone Press,
1710 Roe Crest Drive, North Mankato, Minnesota 56003.
www.capstonepub.com

Books published by Capstone Press are manufactured with paper
containing at least 10 percent post-consumer waste.

Library of Congress Cataloging-in-Publication Data
Scheff, Matt.
    Tom Brady : football superstar / by Matt Scheff.
    p. cm.—(Sports illustrated KIDS. Superstar athletes)
    Includes bibliographical references and index.
    Summary: "Presents the athletic biography of Tom Brady, including his career as a high school and
professional football player"—Provided by publisher.
    ISBN 978-1-4296-7685-4 (library binding)
    ISBN 978-1-4296-8006-6 (paperback)
    1. Brady, Tom, 1977– —Juvenile literature. 2. Football players—United States—
Biography—Juvenile literature. 3. Quarterbacks (Football)—United States—Biography—
Juvenile literature. I. Title.
GV939.B685S39 2011
796.332092—dc23
[B]   2011028640

Editorial Credits
Aaron Sautter, editor; Ted Williams, designer; Eric Gohl, media researcher;
    Laura Manthe, production specialist

Photo Credits
Getty Images/Allsport/Tom Pidgeon, 13; Joe Robbins, 6
Sports Illustrated/Al Tielemans, 15; Andy Hayt, 9; Bill Frakes, cover (right); Bob Rosato, cover (left), 5;
    Damian Strohmeyer, 2¬–3, 10, 18, 21, 22 (bottom), 24; Heinz Kluetmeier, 7, 16, 23; John Biever, 22
    (middle); Peter Read Miller, 22 (top); Robert Beck, 1, 17

Design Elements
Shutterstock/chudo-yudo, designerpix, Fassver Anna, Fazakas Mihaly

Direct Quotations
Page 6, from Associated Press, "New England Shocks St. Louis to Win Super Bowl XXXVI,"
    CNNSI.com, February 3, 2002.
Page 20, from www.associatedcontent.com, November 9, 2009, "The Saving Grace of the New England
    Patriots: Tom Brady Memorable Quotes on Motivation and Success in the NFL," by Alfonso Coley.

Printed in the United States of America in North Mankato, Minnesota.

102011   006405CGS12

TABLE OF CONTENTS

CHAPTER 1

SUPER BOWL SUPERSTAR

On February 3, 2002, the New England Patriots and St. Louis Rams faced off in Super Bowl XXXVI. The two teams were tied 17-17. With less than two minutes left, quarterback Tom Brady led the Patriots onto the field.

Brady was in just his second year in the National Football League (NFL). He'd begun the year as a backup. Few people had thought he'd lead his team to the Super Bowl.

On the team's final drive, Brady completed 5 of 6 passes. He moved the team within **field goal** range. With only a few seconds left, kicker Adam Vinatieri made the deciding field goal.

field goal—a play in which the ball is kicked between the goal posts for three points

The Patriots won! Brady was named the Most Valuable Player (MVP) of the game.

"This is a perfect example of what happens when guys believe in each other." — Tom Brady

CHAPTER 2

ROAD TO THE NFL

Tom Edward Patrick Brady was born August 3, 1977, in San Mateo, California. As a kid, he loved the San Francisco 49ers. His favorite player was quarterback Joe Montana.

Brady played both football and baseball in high school. In 1995 the Montreal Expos **drafted** him to play professional baseball. But he wanted to play football instead.

draft—the process of choosing a person to join a sports team

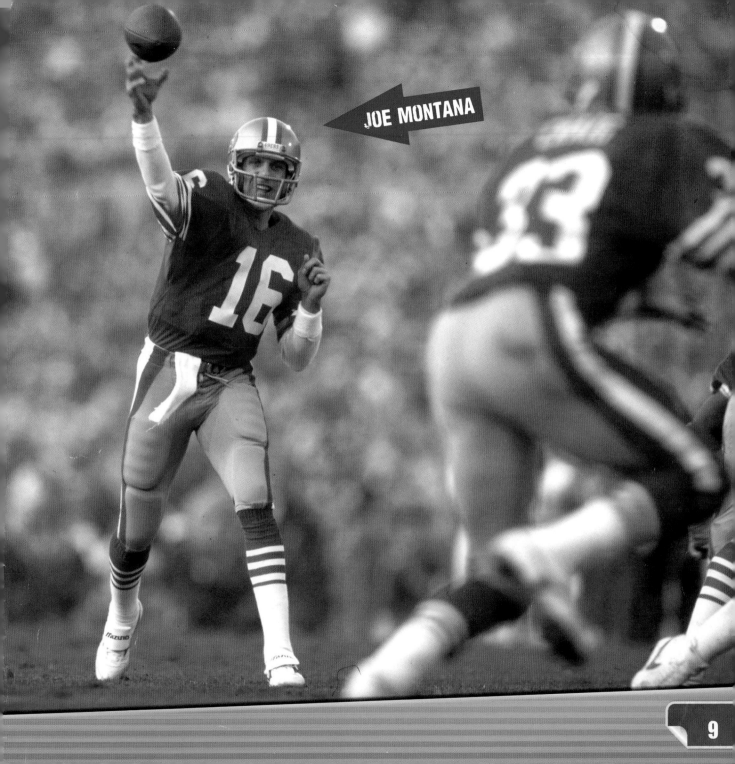

JOE MONTANA

Brady chose to play football at the University of Michigan. In 1997 he was the team's backup quarterback. But he became the starter in 1998 and 1999.

After the 1998 season, he led his team to victory in the Citrus Bowl. His final game was in the 2000 Orange Bowl against Alabama. He led Michigan to a thrilling 35-34 overtime victory.

GIVING HIS ALL

Brady set several records in the 2000 Orange Bowl, including 369 yards passing and four touchdowns. After the game, he was so sore he could barely walk off the field. His dad had to carry his equipment bag for him.

After college, Brady hoped to play for an NFL team. In the 2000 NFL draft, he waited as round after round went by. Brady finally got a call in the sixth round. The New England Patriots had picked him. He was the 199th player chosen.

Brady had to work hard just to make the team. As a **rookie**, he played in only one game. It was a **blowout** loss to the Detroit Lions.

rookie—a first-year player
blowout—a game in which one team greatly outscores the other

CHAPTER 3

NFL STAR

Brady began his NFL career as a backup quarterback. But in 2001 starting quarterback Drew Bledsoe was injured. Brady finally had his chance. He surprised everyone by leading the Patriots to a Super Bowl title.

Brady led the Patriots to a second Super Bowl title after the 2003 season. He was again voted Super Bowl MVP. A year later, the Patriots won a third Super Bowl. In just four years, Brady had already won three championships!

Brady's 2007 season was one to remember. The Patriots were a perfect 16–0 in the regular season. Brady set an NFL record by throwing 50 touchdown passes. He was named the NFL's MVP that year.

In the Super Bowl, the Patriots faced the New York Giants. In the fourth quarter, Brady threw a touchdown pass that gave New England a lead. But the Giants came back to win the game. It was the Patriots' only loss of the year.

In 2008 Brady injured his knee in the first game of the season. He missed the rest of the year. But he came back strong in 2009. He was named NFL Comeback Player of the Year. In 2010 he led the Patriots to a 14–2 record and was again named the NFL's MVP.

TOP QUARTERBACKS

Tom Brady's NFL record 50 touchdown passes in 2007 put him in rare company. Only Peyton Manning, Dan Marino, and Kurt Warner have ever thrown 40 or more touchdowns in a season.

CHAPTER 4

ALL-TIME GREAT

Brady wasn't picked until late in the NFL draft. But he has had great success. He's won three Super Bowls, two Super Bowl MVPs, and two NFL MVPs. Brady started his career as an underdog. But he's become one of the greatest quarterbacks in NFL history.

"Mentally, the only players who survive in the pros are the ones able to manage all their responsibilities."
— Tom Brady

TIMELINE

1977—Tom Brady is born on August 3 in San Mateo, California.

1995—Brady is drafted by MLB's Montreal Expos. He chooses to play football at the University of Michigan instead.

2000—Brady is selected in the sixth round of the NFL draft by the New England Patriots.

2002—Brady leads the Patriots to win Super Bowl XXXVI. He is named Super Bowl MVP.

2004-2005—Brady leads the Patriots to two more Super Bowl titles. He wins a second Super Bowl MVP award.

2007—Brady throws an NFL record 50 touchdown passes. He also leads the Patriots to a 16–0 regular season record and is named NFL MVP.

2010—Brady wins a second NFL MVP award.

GLOSSARY

blowout (BLOW-out)—a game in which one team badly outscores the other

draft (DRAFT)—the process of choosing a person to join a sports team

field goal (FEELD GOHL)—a play in which the ball is kicked through the goalposts for three points

rookie (RUK-ee)—a first-year player

touchdown (TUCH-down)—a play in which a team carries the ball into the opponent's end zone for six points

READ MORE

DiPrimio, Pete. *Tom Brady.* Contemporary Biography. Hockessin, Del.: Mitchell Lane Publishers, 2009.

Doeden, Matt. *The World's Greatest Football Players.* Sports Illustrated Kids. Mankato, Minn.: Capstone Press, 2010.

Savage, Jeff. *Tom Brady.* Amazing Athletes. Minneapolis: Lerner Publications Co., 2009.

INTERNET SITES

FactHound offers a safe, fun way to find Internet sites related to this book. All of the sites on FactHound have been researched by our staff.

Here's all you do:

Visit *www.facthound.com*

Type in this code: 9781429676854

 Check out projects, games and lots more at
www.capstonekids.com

INDEX